STEVE,

Power comes from living in the present moment, where you can take action and create the future.

See you in KAVAI!

Kendall Pugh

Reflections of KAUA'I

AN ISLAND TREASURES BOOK

CHERYL CHEE TSUTSUMI

photographs by

ANN CECIL

 ISLAND HERITAGE

PUBLISHING

Reflections

of KAUA'I

Published and distributed by
ISLAND HERITAGE PUBLISHING

ISBN 0-89610-386-2

Address orders and correspondence to:

ISLAND HERITAGE
PUBLISHING
94-411 Kō'aki Street
Waipahu, Hawai'i 96797
Telephone 800-468-2800
          808-564-8800
www.islandheritage.com

Printed in Hong Kong
First edition, fifth printing, 2002

EDITED BY VIRGINIA WAGEMAN
DESIGNED BY JIM WAGEMAN

Sunset presents
a stunning show
at peaceful
Hanalei Bay.

Contents

Welcome
TO KAUA'I

Think green. Think pristine valleys, magnificent canyons, and soaring peaks. Think taro patches, fragrant gardens, and wide open pastureland. Paint these pictures in your mind and you'll see vignettes of Kaua'i, the oldest of the major Hawaiian islands and arguably the most beautiful.

The Garden Island is, in fact, a 549-square-mile garden in perpetual bloom. At its heart is wet and wild Mount Wai'ale'ale, which is refreshed by rainfall nearly every day of the year. Wai'ale'ale is the centerpiece of a stunning mosaic of meadows, valleys, rain forests, and sheer, furrowed cliffs that defines Kaua'i.

Born a little over 5 1/2 million years ago, Kaua'i has a long and enthralling story to share. It is regarded as the home of the Menehune, a mythical race of small people who would construct aqueducts, fishponds, *heiau* (places of worship), and other imposing works of stone in a single night. Although they stood only about three feet tall, the Menehune were strong, skilled laborers with a very serious work ethic; if they didn't complete a project in one night, it was left forever unfinished.

Spectacular views of the Nā Pali coastline unfold along the Kalalau Trail.

Sunlight and shadows dance on the ridges of Mount Wai'ale'ale.

On a mission to find a Northwest Passage linking the northern Pacific and Atlantic oceans, the intrepid British Captain James Cook spotted the island of O'ahu on January 18, 1778. But instead of dropping anchor off O'ahu, he sailed past it and two days later set foot on Hawaiian soil for the first time in Waimea, on the west coast of Kaua'i. There he was greeted with unrestrained awe and adoration; villagers mistakenly thought he was Lono, the god of peace and fertility.

Cook recorded in his journal entry that day: "As soon as the Ships was [sic] anchored I went ashore with three boats, to look at the water and try the disposition of the inhabitants, several hundreds of whom were assembled on a sandy beach before the Village. The very instant I leaped ashore, they all fell flat on their faces, and remained in that humble posture till I made signs to them to rise."

History books refer to Kaua'i as the "Separate Kingdom," for it was the only major island in the Hawaiian chain that was not conquered by Kamehameha I. As the other islands fell one by one under the great warrior king's rule, Kaua'i alone remained defiant and undefeated. Its king, Kaumuali'i, was firm in his resolve to maintain independence.

*T*his monument (left) marks Waimea as the site where British Captain James Cook first set foot in Hawai'i.

FACING PAGE:
*K*alalau Valley beckons beyond a luxuriant border of ferns at a lookout in Kōke'e State Park.

Fate seemed to be in Kaumuali'i's favor. In 1796 Kamehameha launched an invasion, but many of his war canoes either sank or were severely damaged in a raging storm in the channel between O'ahu and Kaua'i, and he was forced to abort the attack. Eight years later Kamehameha planned another raid on Kaua'i. This time his troops were decimated by a disease, most likely cholera, that had been introduced by Westerners.

In the end Kaua'i was won—but in an unexpected way. After Kamehameha died in 1819, his son, Liholiho, ascended the throne as Kamehameha II. The wily new king invited Kaumuali'i on a cruise aboard his yacht with the intent of kidnapping him. The unsuspecting Kaumuali'i was taken to O'ahu, where he was forced to marry Ka'ahumanu, who had been Kamehameha I's favorite wife. Thus control of Kaua'i was secured and the Hawaiian kingdom united.

The Garden Island's allure has not waned over the centuries. It's no secret that Hollywood loves beautiful Kaua'i. More than sixty movies and television shows have been filmed here since 1933, including *Raiders of the Lost Ark*, *Jurassic Park*, *South Pacific*, and *King Kong*. And now many travelers are discovering what Hollywood filmmakers have known for decades—Kaua'i is indeed a star.

The Noble North
NĀ PALI TO KĪLAUEA

It had been a fruitful night of fishing for the Menehune, the mythical little people who lived in large numbers on Kauaʻi. Before the first rays of sunlight warmed the earth, they gathered and looked with great satisfaction at their huge catch. "We'll dry and salt the fish tonight," they said. "There is enough here for many meals."

After preserving the fish, most of the Menehune retired to their homes in the forest; a few remained behind to stand guard over the precious cache. By now the sun had risen, and the guards started hearing strange sounds—whispering, shuffling, and rocks being moved.

"What are those noises?" the guards wondered. Investigating, they concluded the sounds were not coming from the beach or the mountain slopes. They walked around again, listening more intently.

Then one of the guards solved the mystery. "The sound is coming from the tunnel!" he exclaimed. "There is a narrow tunnel that cuts

Adventure begins where the paved road ends at Kēʻē Beach, near Maniniholo Dry Cave, named for a Menehune chief. This is the gateway to Kauaʻi's famed Nā Pali Coast—twenty-two awe-inspiring miles of fluted cliffs, some soaring three thousand feet above the undulating Pacific. Four pristine valleys—Kalalau, Honopū, Awaʻawapuhi, and Nuʻalolo—are tucked within the bosom of these cliffs. All of the valleys are uninhabited and accessible only by foot, boat, or helicopter.

In these remote regions, the air is seldom stirred by human voices, the earth seldom marred by footprints. It takes even the most seasoned hikers a full day to negotiate the steep, narrow eleven-mile trail

through the mountain. Someone is coming here by crawling through that tunnel!"

Added another guard, "It doesn't sound like just one person, but many! It must be the evil spirits who live on top of the mountain. They've probably seen all the fish we've caught and want to steal them from us. Let's wake up the rest of our comrades and decide what should be done."

When everyone had assembled, their leader Maniniholo spoke: "The evil spirits present a grave danger. Here's a plan. Why don't we cut a corridor into the mountains ourselves? We'll eventually come to the tunnel that the spirits are coming through, and we'll take them by surprise."

The Menehune attended to the task right away, using their tools to dig deep into the side of the mountain. Before long, they reached the passage through which the evil spirits were crawling. As the spirits passed by, the Menehune attacked, killing them all. Thus their life-sustaining supply of fish was saved. The Menehune's tunnel—a large, dry cave that leads to the heart of the mountain—still can be seen in Hā'ena.

A windsurfer takes advantage of brisk north shore breezes.

*T*he late afternoon sun sets the ocean and cliffs of Nā Pali afire.

to Kalalau, the first valley. What they discover at the end of their journey is the "real" Hawai'i—for centuries virtually untouched and unchanged.

The town of Hanalei is fringed with taro patches and cute to the point of being quaint. Despite its down-home demeanor, Hanalei reveals flashes of sophistication. Browse through its boutiques where fabulous buys can be found—handblown glass vases, driftwood sculptures, chic tropical apparel, rattan and koa furniture, one-of-a-kind jewelry.

Boasting splendid views of Hanalei Bay, Princeville is eleven thousand acres of carefully planned opulence. The exclusive resort community encompasses a luxury hotel, single family homes, condominiums, townhouses—and all the amenities that go along with them, including two golf courses, a tennis club, spa and fitness center, shops, stables, and trendy restaurants.

Sugar cane once dominated the landscape and lives of the people in Kīlauea; today the sleepy area's major attractions include Kong Lung, with its amazing inventory of everything from art to aloha wear. "Gump's in the Cane Fields" is the nickname that's been affectionately bestowed upon this stylish store set in the most unlikely of places.

Kīlauea Lighthouse, a National Historical Landmark dating back to 1913, gazes both seaward and inland over the two-hundred-acre Kīlauea Point National Wildlife Refuge. Poised on a promontory 216 feet above crashing waves, the lighthouse would be a lonely figure indeed were it not for the thousands of exotic seabirds that call this sanctuary home. There's nothing quite as exhilarating as tracking red-footed boobies, great frigate birds, and shearwaters in flight, heads held high and wings spread wide in a graceful dance with the clouds.

*S*tone dogs and pillars guard the entrance to Kong Lung in Kīlauea, which carries an intriguing assortment of quality merchandise, including clothing, tableware, and fine art.

*K*ilauea Lighthouse, in use until the mid-1970s, is still a favorite tourist attraction.

*V*isitors to the Princeville Resort area enjoy a tranquil day in paradise.

FAR LEFT:

A visitor to
Hā'ena State Park
watches in awe as
sunset casts a
golden glow over
the Nā Pali Coast.

*T*he paved road
ends near rock-
strewn Kē'ē Beach
at Hā'ena State
Park; from this
point on, Kaua'i's
north shore is all
glorious wilderness.

A formidable
band of green
between blue
sea and blue
sky, Nā Pali
has remained
unchanged for
centuries.

*F*ew people have
ventured into the
rugged hidden
valleys of Nā Pali.

*T*he twin beaches
of Honopū are
cradled by cloud-
wreathed cliffs,
some soaring three
thousand feet high.

*O*cean spray
cools lava rocks
lining Kē'ē Beach.

*C*oconut palms
flourish on the
hill above Kaulu
Paoa, near Kē'ē
Beach, a *heiau* that
once served as a
school for historians
and genealogists.
Nearby is Kaulu
o Laka Heiau,
dedicated to Laka,
goddess of dance,
where hula instruc-
tion once was given.

FACING PAGE:

FACING PAGE:

*S*weethearts stroll along lovely Hā'ena Beach, which is excellent for swimming and snorkeling during the calm summer season.

A snorkeler examines marine life in Hā'ena Beach's crystal clear waters.

FAR LEFT:

*A*ncient *kalo* (taro) terraces are still tended at Limahuli Garden, which was first settled by the Hawaiians about fifteen hundred years ago.

*L*imahuli o Makana in Hāʻena is an option for couples wishing to exchange vows in a beautiful, secluded tropical garden.

*W*ainiha General
Store exudes a
rustic charm.

*I*t's a perfect day
at Y Camp Beach,
near Hā'ena Beach.

*H*analei Bay shows off a shoreline scalloped with cream-colored beaches.

*S*norkelers check out the underwater sights in Hanalei Bay, near Princeville Resort.

FACING PAGE:

*T*he town of
Hanalei retains
the rural feel of
Kauaʻi's north shore.

*S*unday service at
Waioli Huiʻia Church
always draws crowds
of worshipers.
Dating back to 1837,
the neighboring
Waioli Mission
House Museum is
filled with period
furniture, paintings,
books, dishes, and
household items,
including a wooden
butter churn.

PAGES 34–35:

*A*bundant rainfall
makes Hanalei
Valley an ideal
location to grow
taro. The corm
of the taro plant
is cooked and
pounded with
water to make
poi, a staple in
ancient Hawaiʻi.

*K*aua'i supplies about 60 percent of Hawai'i's taro, the majority of which is produced in Hanalei. It is backbreaking work to plant, weed, and harvest taro, which was used to treat a wide variety of ailments in olden times.

If you're seeking
solitude and natural
beauty, Pu'upōā
Beach, below the
resort community
of Princeville, is
one place you'll
find it.

*D*ay yields to night
in dramatic fashion
at Hanalei Bay.
Hanalei Pier (to
the right) was built
in the early 1900s
so that rice, taro,
and other agricul-
tural products
could be shipped
off the island.

*L*ush Princeville
and Hanalei are
just as magnificent
when seen from
the air.

*G*reen surrounds
the green of the
fourteenth hole of
Princeville Resort's
award-winning
Prince Golf Course.

When the sun
and breezes are
out at Hanalei Bay,
so are the sailboats.

The bay is
also a fabulous
playground for
snorkelers.

*H*orses roam verdant pastureland near Princeville (this page) and Kīlauea (facing page). Princeville was named in honor of Prince Albert, the only son of King Kamehameha IV and Queen Emma, after the royal family vacationed at a ranch in the area in 1860. Tragically, the young prince died two years later at the age of four.

'Anini Beach County Park (left) and Secret Beach (right) are among the choices for a quiet north shore escape. In the background is picturesque Kalihiwai Bay (note Kilauea Lighthouse in the distance).

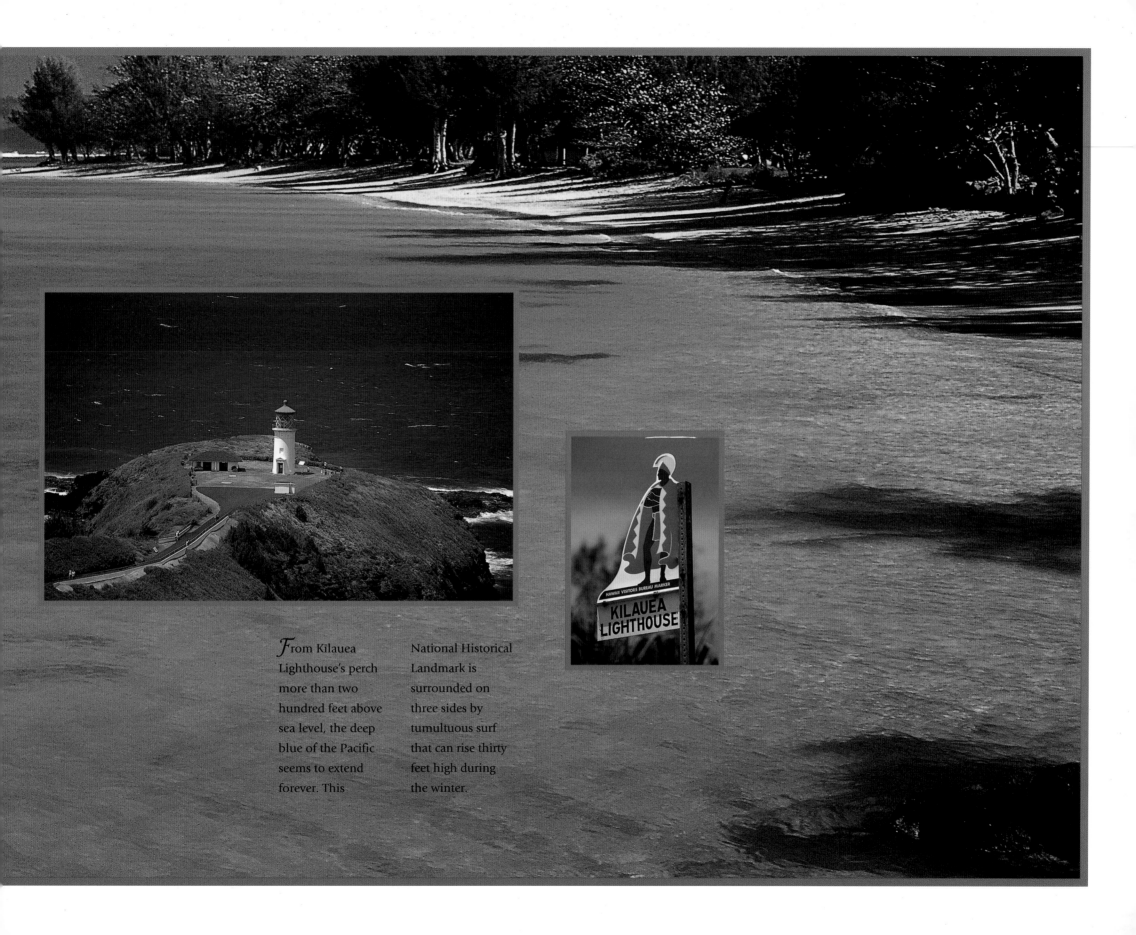

From Kilauea Lighthouse's perch more than two hundred feet above sea level, the deep blue of the Pacific seems to extend forever. This National Historical Landmark is surrounded on three sides by tumultuous surf that can rise thirty feet high during the winter.

*S*miles and flowers
are abundant as
children at Kīlauea
School celebrate
Lei Day (May 1).

Tales and Treasures of the Far East

ANAHOLA TO LĪHUʻE

The twin cascades of Wailua Falls tumble eighty feet into a foliage-lined pool. Long ago, the *aliʻi* (royalty) would dive from the top of the falls into the pool to prove their courage and prowess.

*S*ightseers can clearly see the profile of the Sleeping Giant as they drive along Highway 56 near Kapaʻa.

In days of old, a genial giant named Nunui lived in the area around Wailua and helped the villagers with their daily tasks. Whatever chores needed to be done, the kind-hearted giant always could be counted on to help. When the chief expressed his desire for a heiau *(place of worship) to be constructed, Nunui obliged. He carried massive stones, some weighing several tons, to erect the walls of the* heiau, *and he hauled ʻōhiʻa logs from the mountains to build its interior structures.*

That evening, after consuming a huge feast, the weary Nunui lay down to rest on a nearby mountain. The giant was so tired, he sleeps to this very day on Nounou, which has become popularly known as the Sleeping Giant.

Rugged, regal mountains such as Nounou give Kauaʻi its special character. A prominent landmark on the island's east side, Nounou resembles the profile of a sleeping giant with a protruding stomach and well-defined chin.

Nounou provides an intriguing backdrop for the district of Wailua, which in ancient times was the center of cultural and political activities on Kauaʻi. The Hawaiian royalty favored this fertile area and built many *heiau* here, including Hikina a ka Lā, near the mouth of the Wailua River. This *puʻuhonua* (place of

These scattered rocks in Lydgate State Park near the mouth of the Wailua River are the remnants of Hikina a ka Lā Heiau. This place of worship was built across the river from Wailua Nui a Hoʻāno, where Kauaʻi's kings once landed their canoes.

Restored in 1933, Kalae o ka Manu is one of the oldest *heiau* on Kauaʻi.

refuge) harbored those who had broken a *kapu* (taboo) as well as defeated soldiers during times of war.

Farther west along the Wailua River, Holoholokū Heiau and its adjacent birthing stones are among the most sacred sites in Hawaiʻi. It was imperative that the offspring of Kauaʻi's *aliʻi* (royalty) be born at these birthing stones, or they would lose their high rank. Likewise, if a commoner was able to give birth here, her child was endowed with the status of a chief.

An old saying goes:

Hānau ke aliʻi i loko o Holoholokū, he aliʻi nui;
Hānau ke kanaka i loko o Holoholokū, he aliʻi nō;
Hānau ke aliʻi mawaho aʻe o Holoholokū, ʻaʻohe
    aliʻi he kanaka ia.

The child of a chief born in Holoholokū
    is a high chief;
The child of a commoner born in Holoholokū
    is a chief;
The child of a chief born outside of Holoholokū
    is a commoner.

*L*ocal farmers' prized orchids can be admired and purchased every Friday and Saturday at the Kaua'i Museum.

*S*tately buildings recall Kaua'i's past (clockwise from top left): Grove Farm Homestead, dating back to 1864; the Kaua'i Museum, which was originally dedicated in 1924 as a public library; and Kilohana, built in 1935 as the centerpiece of a vast sugar plantation. Horse-drawn carriage rides through the estate are a fun diversion.

Nature has strewn her own wonders in Wailua, including the Fern Grotto, a magnificent cavern that's draped with an abundance of hanging ferns, and Keāhua Arboretum, a lush haven pierced by an ancient trail that leads to Mount Wai'ale'ale. Centuries ago, the Hawaiians made annual pilgrimages up Wai'ale'ale to honor Kāne, the god of creation, sunlight, fresh water, and forests. The *Guinness Book of Records* lists Wai'ale'ale as the area with the most rainy days (up to 350) per year. Appropriately, its name means "overflowing water."

South of Wailua is Līhu'e, Kaua'i's unpretentious county seat, which might go unnoticed save for such attractions as Grove Farm Homestead, once a flourishing sugar plantation; the Kaua'i Museum, with its fascinating exhibits of koa furniture, quilts, shells, weapons, *kapa* (tapa), and other Hawaiiana; and Kilohana, a stately Tudor-style manor built in 1935 by sugar magnate Gaylord Wilcox.

The 'Alakoko Fishpond, often called the Menehune Fishpond, draws sightseers to the quiet adjacent community of Niumalu. At the request of a
Kaua'i chief, so legend goes, the industrious Menehune (a legendary race of small people) consented
to build this pond overnight on one condition: that
no one watch them while they worked. The chief
agreed to the unusual terms at first, but he got more
and more curious as he heard the Menehune moving,
chiseling, and fitting stones into place. Unable to
resist the urge, he moved aside some thatch in his
hale (house) to sneak a peek.

The leader of the Menehune immediately knew the
chief had broken his promise, and he instructed his
people to stop all work on the project. Before return-
ing home the Menehune washed their hands—bleeding
from cuts made by the rough stones they had been
carrying—in the nearly completed pond that now
bears the chief's name: 'Alakoko or "rippling blood."

FACING PAGE:
*M*ullet are
raised in the
900-foot-long
'Alakoko Fishpond,
which legend
says was built by
the Menehune.

*N*ature is a
wonderful
companion at
Anahola Beach
County Park.

Coconut palms tower over homes in Kapa'a.

Youths prepare the *imu* (underground oven) and pig for a luau at the Kaua'i Coconut Beach Resort.

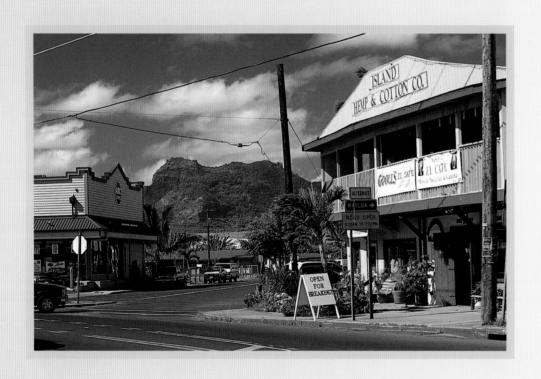

FACING PAGE:

*O*ld storefronts
imbue Kapa'a with
a nostalgic air (left),
as does the modest
plantation home
that has been
transformed into
a gallery (right).

*O*rnamental shrubs
bloom profusely
on the Garden Isle
of Kaua'i, like this
brilliant red and
yellow *'ohai ali'i*,
literally, royal *'ohai*.

*A*ll of sacred Wailua is captured in this breath-taking panorama.

*B*alanced on slippery rocks at Wailua Beach, a fisherman gets set to throw his net.

*G*raceful waterfalls add to the east side's allure, among them 'Ōpaeka'a Falls and Wailua Falls (facing page). From a lookout across the road from 'Ōpaeka'a Falls, you can enjoy a dramatic view of Kamōkila Hawaiian Village, where opening scenes in the movie *Outbreak*, starring Dustin Hoffman, were filmed.

*M*otorized
barges transport
visitors two miles
up the Wailua River
to the Fern Grotto
(left), a popular
wedding site.

A great family escape, Lydgate State Park provides sheltered picnic tables; barbecue grills; a playground complete with swings, slides, and sandboxes; and a beautiful beach.

A tour boat cruises along the forested banks of the Wailua River on its way to the Fern Grotto.

*M*orning traffic jams a main artery in Lihuʻe, Kauaʻi's county seat.

A truck loaded with sugar cane is ready to head to Lihuʻe Plantation Company's mill for processing.

*P*leasure boats bob in their berths at Nāwiliwili Harbor.

*O*ffering interisland cruise vacations, the SS *Independence* makes weekly calls at Nāwiliwili.

*S*urfers check out the waves at Kalapaki Beach, which fronts the Kaua'i Marriott Resort and Beach Club.

*W*armed by the late afternoon sun, golfers plan their strategy at the thirteenth hole of Kaua'i Lagoons' award-winning Kiele Course, which was designed by Jack Nicklaus.

Southern Beauty
PO'IPŪ TO HANAPĒPĒ

Bright red jade vines bloom along Lāwa'i Stream at Allerton Garden.

Po'ipū claims its own Old Faithful—Spouting Horn, where energetic wave action forces seawater up through a lava tube as high as fifty feet in the air.

Kaikapu was a mo'o *(dragon) who was well known throughout Kaua'i for her ferocious appetite and fiery temper. She would hide behind rocks, waiting for her prey—fishermen who were foolish enough to lay their traps, nets, and lines along the shore. As word spread about the menacing* mo'o, *the area where she lived on Kaua'i's south shore became deserted.*

One day a young boy named Liko thought of bringing his grandmother some hīnālea *(wrasse, a colorful marine fish). He knew* hīnālea *thrived along the coast where the dreaded Kaikapu lived, but he decided to be daring.*

With his fish traps grasped firmly in his hands, Liko took a deep breath and jumped into the ocean. In a moment Kaikapu was by his side, her jaws wide open, ready to devour him. Being small

Spouting Horn is just one of the many lures of the sunny south shore, which reigns as Kaua'i's most popular visitor destination. Hawai'i's sugar industry was born in Kōloa; the first plantation, Kōloa Sugar Plantation, was established here in 1835. A weathered stone chimney in a grassy field is all that remains of the original plantation.

In Po'ipū, a manicured acre facing the sea marks the birthplace of Prince Jonah Kūhiō Kalaniana'ole, Hawai'i's second territorial delegate to the U.S. Congress. Terraced lava rock walls, a fishpond, a profusion of palms, and a monument that's usually adorned with fresh flower leis make this park a perfect spot for picnicking and daydreaming.

and lithe, Liko nimbly dodged her and swam into an underwater lava tube that led from the sea to land.

Enraged, Kaikapu followed him, but she was so big she became stuck in the lava tube. The harder she struggled to free herself, the more tightly she became wedged. And there she remains today. The bellow that's heard as water shoots more than fifty feet skyward through the lava tube at Spouting Horn is emitted by the frustrated and angry Kaikapu.

There's no question that nature stars on southern Kaua'i's stage. Po'ipū Resort wears a lei of lovely beaches; within a one-mile stretch of picturesque coastline, water babies can indulge in a literal ocean of activities, including swimming, boogie-boarding, surfing, snorkeling, and diving. Accommodations, ranging from cozy bed-and-breakfasts to posh hotels, are clustered along the shore, right where all the action is.

Long ago the Hawaiians also lived and played here in great numbers. Po'ipū has yielded a trove of archaeological gems dating back hundreds of years, including walls and platforms of house sites, lava tube shelters, burial grounds, irrigation ditches, petroglyphs, fishing shrines, and a *heiau* (place of worship).

Lāwa'i and Allerton gardens, part of the National Tropical Botanical Garden, and Moir Garden at Kiahuna Plantation are Kaua'i's visions of Eden.

Thousands of varieties of tropical plants, flowers, and trees delight the senses and serve as exquisite subjects for photos.

On the outskirts of Hanapēpē, salt ponds—shallow basins dug into the red earth in the seventeenth century—still are used by *kama'āina* (local residents) during the spring and summer months when the sun is strong enough to evaporate seawater, leaving mounds of shimmering salt crystals. This is a worthwhile stop to make before meandering through Hanapēpē itself.

In Kaua'i's "Biggest Little Town," vintage buildings house wonderful art galleries, restaurants, and shops, making a visit of a few hours pass very quickly. Pick out a painting of a rustic Kaua'i scene; try on a bright pareu; or lick a *pohā* berry, banana, or coconut ice cream cone. Hanapēpē is a colorful palette of local-style living and a nostalgic slice of early-1900s Kaua'i, neatly frozen in time.

*I*slanders evaporate
seawater in these
shallow basins at
Salt Pond Beach
County Park to
produce salt
crystals, just as
the Hawaiians
did three hundred
years ago.

*T*he clock seems
to have stopped
ticking decades
ago in Hanapēpē,
Kaua'i's "Biggest
Little Town."

PAGES 80–81:
*T*his bird's-eye
view of the Hā'upu
(Hoary Head) Ridge
reveals an ocean
of green.

Over a mile of Maluhia Road, which leads to Kōloa town, is shaded by a tunnel of fragrant eucalyptus trees.

A snorkeler catches a glimpse of the underwater world at Poʻipū Beach Park.

Friends frolic in the surf off Poʻipū Beach.

*T*he golden sands
of Shipwreck Beach
front the Hyatt
Regency Kaua'i
in Po'ipū.

*S*urfers challenge
the waves at Ship-
wreck Beach.

A plump Hawaiian
monk seal, which
is on the list of
endangered species,
lounges on the
warm sands of
Po'ipū Beach.

*S*hipwreck Beach is a picturesque spot to read, sun, and daydream.

*T*he one-hundred-acre Allerton Garden in Lāwa'i is part of the National Tropical Botanical Garden, which was chartered by Congress in 1964. One of Queen Emma's summer vacation homes originally stood on the site, and she planted the first seedlings for her garden there in the 1870s.

FACING PAGE:

*W*aves crash against
the rocky coastline
of Keoneloa Bay
in Po'ipū.

*V*isitors explore
Kaua'i's scenic
southern shore
on horseback.

*S*unset paints
the sky above the
Sheraton Kaua'i and
the tide pools of
Kukui'ula Bay with
amber and gold.

FAR LEFT:

*N*ature maintains a commanding presence in the rural Kalāheo area.

*W*insome Kōloa (this page) was the site of the first sugar plantation in Hawai'i. Each July, Kōloa Plantation Days celebrate that distinction with a weeklong series of events, including a music festival, block party, rodeo, ocean sports competitions, and Hawaiian entertainment.

Simple, quiet, and easygoing define life in Hanapēpē town.

With majestic mountains as a backdrop, cattle graze contentedly in the lush meadows of Kalāheo.

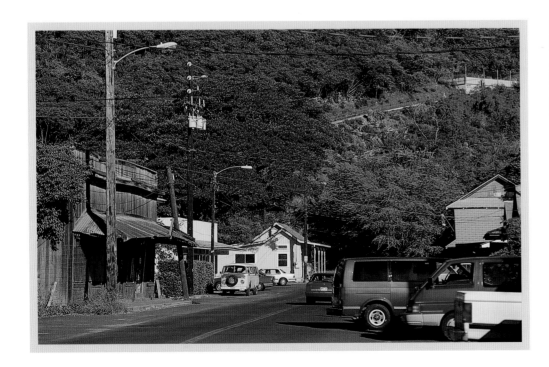

West Side Story

Peace and beauty envelop a hiker in Kōke'e State Park.

The myriad hues of sunset swirl around Kalalau Valley.

High up in the mountains of Kōke'e, there is a section of land where plants never grow. This is very unusual, for the rest of Kōke'e is blanketed with thick, fragrant forest.

Long ago, so legend goes, a man named Kamaka grew taro, sugar cane, bananas, and sweet potatoes on this now-barren site. Kamaka usually produced more crops than he and his family could eat, but he never shared any of the food. If a hungry passerby stopped and asked for a bite to eat, Kamaka's response was always unkind: "Away with you! We have just enough for ourselves."

One evening a giant stopped by Kamaka's home. He was on his way back to his mountain cave when the afternoon mist drifted in, causing him to lose his way. After hours of wandering, he was tired, hungry, and looking forward to settling down for the night.

In a word, west Kaua'i is extraordinary. The range in climate here is astounding—from warm and dry along the sun-splashed shore to cool and moist more than four thousand feet above sea level in the verdant mountain regions.

Forty-five miles of well-marked, well-maintained trails crisscross Kōke'e State Park, 4,345 acres of wilderness perfumed with native plants such as **maile, mokihana, 'ōhi'a lehua,** and **iliau.** The trails vary greatly in terms of length and difficulty, from easy strolls that young children and the elderly can enjoy to rugged day-long treks that require slogging through knee-deep bog. Many endangered native Hawaiian birds and plants thrive in the ten-square-mile Alaka'i Swamp, the state's largest swamp, which borders Kōke'e.

"Aloha!" the giant called out. "Can you offer food and shelter to a weary traveler?"

Kamaka peered out from the doorway of his hut and, in his usual ungracious manner, snapped, "Begone! We have nothing to give to beggars!"

The giant left and walked to the edge of the forest where he lay down, hoping to get some sleep beneath a canopy of trees. But during the night a heavy rain fell, leaving him drenched, cold, and miserable. When daylight came, the giant was able to make his way home, but he was furious. He wanted to teach inconsiderate Kamaka a lesson!

That night he returned to Kamaka's garden and under the cover of darkness executed his revenge. When Kamaka woke the next morning, he found all of his crops had been uprooted. From then on, if Kamaka planted anything, the giant would come at night and dig up the seeds and young shoots. And so to this day nothing has ever grown again in the place in Kōke'e where stingy Kamaka's garden once flourished.

A fifteen-minute drive from Kōke'e, Waimea Canyon is a remarkable example of nature's handiwork. Mark Twain dubbed it the "Grand Canyon of the Pacific," and grand it is—3,600 feet deep, one mile wide, and ten miles long. Rainbows, shadows, and drifting clouds create striking patterns that transform the mood and look of the chasm in minutes. Although Waimea Canyon is magnificent at any hour, it is most dramatic at the end of the day, when sunset imbues its rich earth tones with an ethereal beauty.

The town of Waimea is surprisingly modest about its role more than two centuries ago as Captain Cook's first landing site in Hawai'i. Only two simple markers, one near a county park and the other on a median strip in the center of town, make note of this historic event. But that's exactly Waimea's style—laid-back and low-key.

Waimea's Menehune Ditch is an amazing feat of engineering. An ancient aqueduct that's still used to irrigate taro fields, it is constructed of hand-hewn

The Menehune Ditch is yet another incredible feat of engineering and hydraulics attributed to the legendary "little people" of Kaua'i.

Sweethearts go for a dip in the waters off Polihale Beach, one of the widest and longest beaches in all of Hawai'i.

stones, neatly and tightly fitted together with no mortar. Stories handed down orally through the generations say Ola, a high chief of Waimea, contracted the Menehune, a mythical race of small people, to do the job. As usual, the strong, efficient workers finished it in a single night, and Ola paid them in 'ōpae, the tiny shrimp that was their staple. The Hawaiian name for the ditch is Kīkī a Ola, literally, "the container acquired by Ola."

Three miles long and three hundred feet wide, Polihale is one of nature's marvels. Sand dunes crowned with vegetation rise as high as one hundred feet, blessing the beach, which ranks among Hawai'i's largest, with contours and textures seldom seen anywhere else in the state. At midday the sands of Polihale are as white and hot as the Sahara's. It's difficult to imagine that just around a bend in the coastline stand the westernmost ramparts of lofty, luxuriant Nā Pali.

FAR LEFT:
*W*aterfalls plummet
from rugged cliffs,
eventually feeding
the Waimea River,
which flows through
Waimea Canyon.

*W*aimea town's
main street is
bordered by
modest shops
and restaurants.

*N*estled oceanfront
in a grove of palms,
Waimea Plantation
Cottages are restored
sugar plantation
cottages dating
from the 1880s
to the 1930s.

*O*ver the centuries
the elements have
eroded a fault in the
Earth's crust into
the gaping gorge
known as Waimea
Canyon.

PAGES 104–105:
*T*he "Grand Canyon
of the Pacific" is a
montage of crags,
buttes, and ridges
showing off breath-
taking textures
and colors that
change with each
movement of the
sun and clouds.

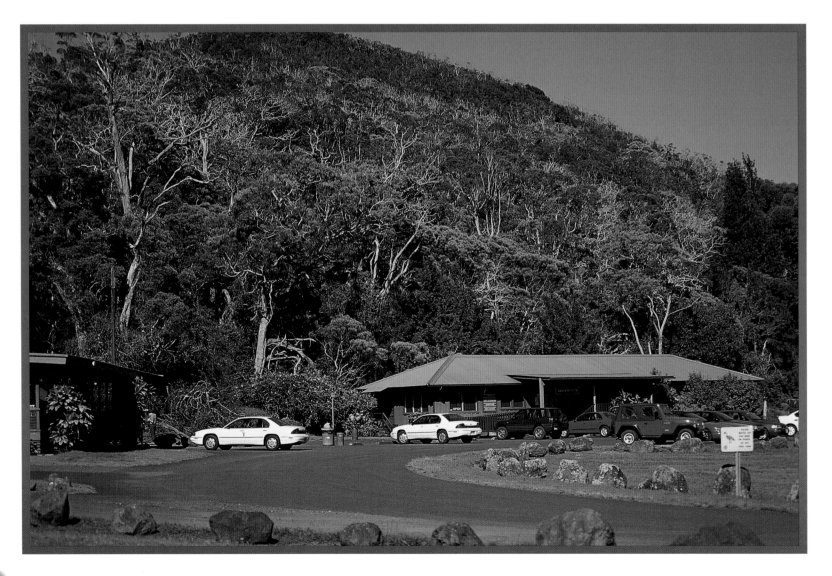

*K*ōke'e State Park is a haven for the *nēnē*, or Hawaiian goose, Hawai'i's state bird.

*C*ozy but definitely worthwhile, Kōke'e Natural History Museum features exhibits about the geology, plants, and animals in the region; detailed maps of the park's forty-five-mile network of trails; and a nice selection of Hawaiiana books.

*M*ist shrouds
hikers on their trek
through a rain
forest in Kōke'e.

A young visitor
plays with a flock
of *moa*, red jungle
chickens, which
congregate near
Kōke'e Lodge.

FAR LEFT:

A family hike on Kōke'e's Pihea Trail culminates with this spectacular view of Kalalau Valley.

*T*he *'ōhi'a lehua* flourishes in cool Kōke'e, a vast wilderness sprawled over 4,345 acres, four thousand feet above sea level. The early Hawaiians used the tree's hard wood to make religious images, spears, and mallets.

A couple washes away the cares of the day with a sunset swim at Kekaha Beach (right). The island of Niʻihau is in the distance.

A bonfire warms picnickers at Kekaha Beach at sunset (facing page)—a perfect way to end a day on Kauaʻi.

*K*ekaha Beach offers miles of sand for horseback riding.

References

Bisignani, J. D. *Hawaii Handbook: The All Island Guide.* Chico, Calif.: Moon Publications, 1995.

———. *Kauai Handbook.* Chico, Calif.: Moon Publications, 1997.

Foster, Jeanette, and Jocelyn Fujii. *Frommer's 99 Hawaii.* New York: Simon and Schuster, 1998.

Pūku'i, Mary Kawena, comp. *Tales of the Menehune.* Honolulu: Kamehameha Schools Bernice Pauahi Bishop Estate, 1994.

———. *The Water of Kāne and Other Legends of the Hawaiian Islands.* Honolulu: Kamehameha Schools Bernice Pauahi Bishop Estate, 1994.

Tregaskis, Moana. *Hawai'i.* Oakland, Calif.: Compass American Guides, 1998.

Wichman, Frederick B. *Kaua'i: Ancient Place-Names and Their Stories.* Honolulu: University of Hawai'i Press, 1998.